Love,
The Hor
famil

MW00412313

College Cooking 101:
Fast Food Without a Kitchen

This book is dedicated to my dad who always loved cooking and trying out new recipes on us. His life will always be an inspiration to mine.

I want to acknowledge my college student and my other soon-to-be college student – you both inspire me and have truly been my muse for writing this book. To my husband – thank you for believing in me and supporting all my dreams, including this book. Life is so much sweeter sharing it with your biggest cheerleader. To my baby girl – your creativity and love make my life richer. And last, but not least, thank you to my mom who brought comfort to my life through food and many other ways as well. May this book comfort students away from home and remind them of home cooking and the love baked inside.

How This Book Was Born

When my oldest child went away to college we bought her the most expensive "all access" meal plan with unlimited swipes. We toured the campus and the cafeteria seemed so inviting with all of its choices. I figured she would eat three meals a day there plus drop in for snacks occasionally. The reality proved to be a much different scenario. The cafeteria lines were generally very long and it took quite a while to actually get the food and eat it. Depending on her class schedule and how far away her class was from the cafeteria, she was sometimes concerned she could not eat quickly enough to make it to class on time. Breakfast was one meal that was definitely not happening in the cafeteria. Eating there would have meant getting up at least an hour early to walk and stand in line and sleep is just too precious to a college student. When she did eat there, the meals didn't taste like home and they didn't always have what she was craving. It became clear pretty quickly that she was going to have to begin cooking in her dorm room. There are no kitchens in the average college dorm so a little ingenuity was needed. That is where this book begins…

Preface

To the college student reading this book:

Welcome to a very exciting time in your life. It is my sincere hope that you will find a little piece of home in this book as you bite into a chicken sandwich like your mom used to make. Our greatest senses are smell and taste and it's amazing how a home-cooked meal can bring us happiness by triggering them.

Fast food restaurants (many of which are appearing on college campuses) are a fun treat that no doubt you will enjoy. I would caution you to limit your trips to them. Nothing will put the extra pounds known as the dreaded "freshman 15" on faster and will make you more tired and leave you wanting to eat more. Eating out often will leave your clothes tight and your wallet thin. One of the worst things about eating fast food is that it's full of unknown ingredients and added preservatives (chemicals, essentially). This book gives you recipes to make the foods you would get at a restaurant but in your room with familiar ingredients.

I've divided this book into sections by cooking appliance. You may want to start small and purchase just a couple of these devices. The back of the book has some great healthy suggestions to keep in the dorm for a study snack or a pick-me-up between meals. If a small refrigerator is not provided in your dorm room, I suggest you buy or rent one. It is necessary for storing several important items.

All of these recipes are designed to serve one or two. Remember, for the dishes that call for meat, you can go to the meat counter at a grocery store and ask the butcher for smaller portions, like one chicken breast or ¼ pound of ground beef. You do not have to buy the packages that have way more than what you need. The recipes are all catered to what you like, fast food, but made at home (your new home, that is) with real ingredients. I've tried to cover all your favorites in this book such as copycat Chick-Fil-A, cheeseburgers, nachos, tacos, Thai take out and pumpkin lattes.

Use this book to make your dorm or apartment feel like home. Invite a few friends over for quesadillas or indoor s'mores for something a little different. Make your roommate a mug cake on his or her birthday. Let this book be one of the essentials you pack for school. These recipes are designed to be QUICK and EASY as I know you'd rather spend your time studying or sleeping than cooking.

There is also a list in the back of this book of everything you need to buy for a dorm room. This list is very comprehensive and includes items such as an umbrella and cold medicine that most people would not think about but are essential to have in a pinch.

Enjoy your college years . . . bon appétit!

Table of Contents

Microwave

Many dorm rooms are now equipped with micro-waves or have one provided for the floor at a central location. They make heating up meals and snacks a snap. These recipes have been tested for cook time with a standard microwave (typically 1000-1200 watts). If your microwave is on the smaller side it may have lower wattage and take longer to cook. If it is not cooked after the time shown in the recipe, add cook time in 15 or 30 second intervals.

Blueberry Pancake in a Mug

If you don't like blueberries just omit them for a buttermilk pancake in a mug! Strawberries work well too.

½ cup complete pancake mix
½ cup milk or water (milk makes this better!)
Several blueberries (fresh or frozen that have been thawed)
Butter
Pancake/maple syrup

Combine pancake mix and milk/water in a mug and mix well. Add the fruit on top. Cook for 1½ minutes in microwave. Add a pat of butter and syrup.

Loaded Baked Potato

This makes the perfect meal for lunch or dinner.

1 medium Idaho or russet potato
2 strips of crumbled bacon
Few pieces of broccoli
Teaspoon of butter
Few pinches of shredded or sliced cheddar cheese

Cook 2 slices of bacon in the microwave on high for 1½ to 2 minutes until done. (To cook bacon in the microwave, place the strips on a microwave safe plate with three paper towels underneath the meat and two paper towels on top.) Remove from microwave and cook a few pieces of broccoli for 30 seconds.

Poke a potato with a fork and wrap in a wet paper towel. Place on plate and microwave on high for 7 minutes.

Using care as it will be hot, slice the potato open lengthwise and add butter, cooked bacon, broccoli and cheddar cheese. Microwave 20 more seconds.

Western Omelet in a Mug

Eat this on your way to class to give you the energy you need to face the day!

1 egg
1 tablespoon diced ham or one slice of chopped deli ham
1 tablespoon green pepper
1 ½ tablespoons grated cheddar cheese
Cooking oil spray

Spray the mug with cooking oil spray so the omelet will not stick. Crack the egg into the mug and mix well with 1 tablespoon of water. Add ham, peppers, cheese and stir again. Cook 30 seconds and stir, then cook another 30 seconds. It should not be runny but fully formed. The omelet will come out of the mug round, so it is perfect on a bagel or English muffin.

Chicago Pizza in a Mug

There is nothing quite like Chicago style pizza with its thick crust and gooey cheese. This is great for lunch or dinner or to power you through those late nights studying.

¼ cup flour
⅛ teaspoon baking soda
⅛ teaspoon baking powder
⅛ teaspoon salt
3 tablespoons milk or water
1 ¼ teaspoon olive oil
2 ¼ tablespoons pizza or spaghetti sauce
1 ½ tablespoons shredded mozzarella cheese
2 pieces of pepperoni (cut each into 4 pieces)
¼ teaspoon Italian seasoning

Add the first 6 ingredients to the mug and mix well. Layer the sauce, cheese, pepperoni and Italian seasoning on top. Microwave for 1 minute and 10 seconds or cheese completely melts.

Mexican Bowl (Vegetarian Style)

You know those pricey little Mexican restaurants with the yummy rice and veggie bowls? Yep, they are great and you can make them at home so simply!

1 cup of brown or jasmine rice (buy some that is already cooked and just needs to be microwaved such as Uncle Ben's Ready Rice)
¼ cup black beans (drained from can)
¼ cup corn (drained from can)
2 tablespoons salsa
1 tablespoon plain Greek yogurt
4 tablespoons shredded cheddar

Prepare rice in the microwave and cook according to package directions. In a microwave safe bowl place all of the above ingredients (including cooked rice) and stir. Cook on high 45 seconds or until all the cheese is melted. This is really great to top with cilantro or fresh avocado.

BLT (Bacon, Lettuce and Tomato) Sandwich

You did your own laundry today and you deserve to be treated to a fantastic meal like this one!

3 strips of uncooked bacon
Leaf or romaine lettuce
Tomato

Mayonnaise
Bread of your choice
Paper towels

Place 3 strips of bacon on top of 3 paper towels on a microwave safe plate. Cover with 2 more sheets of paper towels and cook on high for about 2 minutes. Toast bread if possible, then add mayonnaise, cooked bacon, lettuce and tomato.

Chili for One

There is nothing like a bowl of chili to remind you of home on a cold winter day. Grab some extra packages of crackers the next time you are in the cafeteria to enjoy with this. I put the leftover beans and tomato sauce in small zipper seal bags in the fridge to enjoy for the next day.

3 tablespoons canned hot chili beans
3 tablespoons canned black beans
½ tablespoon chopped onion
6 tablespoons tomato sauce
¾ teaspoon chili powder
¼ teaspoon cumin
1 teaspoon sugar
Dash of pepper

Place all ingredients in a mug and mix. Heat for about 1 minute.

Mug Cake

Make this for your roommate's birthday or for yourself after that hard-won "A" on a research paper!

1½ tablespoons of angel food cake mix
1½ tablespoons of any other flavor cake mix (chocolate, vanilla, etc.)
2 tablespoons water
Prepared frosting (buy a container, add the amount
  you like and save the rest for next time)

Mix the first three ingredients in a mug and stir well.
Microwave 1 minute on high.

Add frosting and enjoy!

Sarah H. Long

Microwave Nachos

Instead of ordering pizza, invite your friends over for a late-night study break with nachos!

Tortilla chips
1 cup refried beans
4 tablespoons canned diced tomatoes and green chilies
2 cups Mexican blend cheese
Toppings of guacamole, sour cream and salsa

Scatter tortilla chips on microwave-safe plate. Place beans and tomatoes on top of chips and microwave 30 seconds. Add shredded cheese and microwave 1 additional minute. Add toppings of your choice.

Scrambled Eggs

This is a "must have" recipe for any college student. Since this makes the egg take on the circular shape of the mug, use this to make a breakfast sandwich on the go with toast/croissants/English muffins and some bacon/sausage/Canadian bacon and a slice of cheese!

2 eggs

1 tablespoon milk or water
Cooking spray or butter
Salt/pepper (grab some packets from the cafeteria to
    keep in your room!)

Butter the inside of a mug or spray it with cooking
oil. Using a fork, combine the eggs with the milk or
water until the egg is well mixed. Throw in a dash of
salt and pepper, if desired. Microwave for 1½
minutes, stirring halfway through the cooking time.
It should look firm and not liquid-like at all.

Mom's Meatloaf in a Mug

Didn't score as well as you'd hoped on a test? You may be in need of some comfort food. This makes a great sandwich too; just add your favorite bun or roll.

¼ pound ground chuck
1 ½ tablespoons of quick oats
1 tablespoon ketchup
1 ½ tablespoons milk
¾ teaspoon onion soup mix
½ tablespoon diced green pepper

Mix all ingredients together well and cook for 3 minutes or until no longer pink in the middle. Top with extra ketchup if desired.

Macaroni and Cheese

This is so easy and made with whole ingredients instead of the artificial stuff contained in the pre-made variety.

½ cup elbow macaroni or small shell pasta

½ cup water
⅛ teaspoon salt
¼ cup milk
½ cup shredded cheddar

Combine pasta, water and salt in a mug and cook 2 minutes. Add another tablespoon of water and stir well to combine. Continue cooking until pasta is fully cooked (I cook 4 additional minutes removing the mug after each minute of cooking to make sure there is still enough water in the bottom of the mug to cover the noodles during cooking. I usually have to add another tablespoon of water in the middle of this 4 minute cooking time. When it is done there should be no water and the pasta soft.) Stir again and add milk and cheese, cook another minute.

French Toast

This is the perfect breakfast and cooks in a little over a minute.

2 slices of bread, torn into pieces or cubed
1 tablespoon butter
1 egg
3 tablespoons milk
Dash of cinnamon
Pancake/maple syrup

Melt butter in a mug for 25 seconds in the microwave. In a separate bowl, combine egg, milk, cinnamon and stir. Put bread in mug with butter and pour egg and milk mixture over both and stir. Microwave 1 minute and 15 seconds (egg should not be runny) and add syrup.

Penne Pasta with Marinara

Yes, you can make pasta in the microwave! Serve with bread and a salad and dinner is ready!

¼ cup penne pasta
2 tablespoons of spaghetti sauce
Shredded mozzarella cheese

Put ¼ cup penne pasta in a mug with ½ cup water. Heat in the microwave for 2 minutes. Stir, add ¼ cup more water and microwave 4 more minutes until pasta is cooked (soft). Drain. Add 2 tablespoons of spaghetti sauce and sprinkle mozzarella on top. Microwave for 30 more seconds.

Roasted Granola

This tastes just like it was roasted in the oven. Perfect served with yogurt and fruit (fresh or dried like raisins and cranberries).

1 tablespoon pancake syrup or agave
2 teaspoons water
2 teaspoons coconut, canola or vegetable oil
⅛ teaspoon salt
¼ cup old fashioned oats
2 tablespoons chopped nuts and/or seeds of your choice (I like almonds, pecans and sunflower seeds)

Mix all ingredients in mug and cook 1 minute 30 seconds. Stir well then cook 1 more minute until golden brown, being careful to check it every 15 seconds so it doesn't burn. Let cool a few minutes before eating.

Electric Skillet

The electric skillet is probably my favorite as it is the most versatile appliance for dorm room cooking. It operates just as if you were cooking on a stovetop with a skillet. The non-stick and copper ones make cleaning the appliance after a meal very easy. If you move into an apartment, these recipes will work in a regular skillet as well.

Chicken Quesadillas with Homemade Guacamole

2 tablespoons vegetable oil
2 tablespoons red wine vinegar
½ teaspoon sugar
½ teaspoon oregano
½ teaspoon chili powder
¼ teaspoon garlic powder
¼ teaspoon salt
1 chicken breast, sliced
Cooking spray
2 tablespoons diced green pepper
½ cup shredded cheddar cheese
Tortillas
Salsa to dip, if desired

Mix together first 7 ingredients in a bowl or zipper seal bag and marinate chicken for at least ½ hour. Heat the electric skillet to 350°F. Add another tablespoon of oil and cook chicken for 5 minutes, tossing a few times while cooking to make sure it's cooked on all sides. Set chicken aside and clean out skillet. Spray skillet with cooking spray and place one tortilla in skillet. Layer tortilla with chicken, green pepper and cheese. Top with second tortilla and spray cooking oil on top. Cook approximately 3 to 4 minutes (using spatula to flip about every 30 seconds so it does not burn but gets brown/crisp and cheese is melted).

Homemade Guacamole

1 ripe avocado (firm but gives slightly to touch)
$\frac{1}{8}$ teaspoon salt (or a pinch)
$\frac{1}{2}$ teaspoon lime juice

Cut avocado in half. Scrape the inside of both avocado halves into bowl discarding the outside shells and pit. Add salt and lime juice and mash together with a fork.

Soft Tacos (or Taco Salad)

Invite your friends over for Taco Tuesday! This recipe makes enough for about 4 hungry people.

Tortillas
½ pound ground chuck
2 tablespoons of taco seasoning (about ½ packet)
⅓ cup water
Shredded cheddar cheese
Iceberg lettuce (cut in pieces)
Salsa

Heat electric skillet to 350°F. Cook ground chuck for about 8 minutes until no longer pink. Use a spatula to flip the meat in order to cook evenly every minute or so. Drain excess oil. Add taco seasoning and ⅓ cup of water and cook an additional 2 minutes. Serve with tortillas and toppings of choice or over lettuce to make a taco salad.

Sarah H. Long

Cheeseburger

I think every college student has had to call mom and ask how to cook a basic cheeseburger. You're welcome...

¼ pound ground round hamburger

Slice of cheese (American, cheddar, or whatever you like)

Montreal steak seasoning (this is mostly a salt and pepper mix)

Hamburger buns

Ketchup, mustard, mayo, lettuce if desired (see if you can grab some extra packets from the cafeteria to keep on hand)

4 tablespoons butter

Turn skillet to 350°F. Mix together hamburger and ¼ tablespoon Montreal steak seasoning and form into a patty. Coat skillet with 2 tablespoons of butter. Place in skillet and cover for 10 minutes, flipping burger a couple times during cooking. Don't press the burger as it will not be as moist if you squeeze the juice out. Turn heat down to simmer and place cheese on top of burger to melt. Put burger onto plate and drain juice out of skillet. Melt another 2 tablespoons of butter. Place buns in butter face down to toast for 1 minute. Assemble burger and enjoy!

Chicken Enchilada Skillet Meal

My older daughter loves enchiladas. These are easy enough for her to make any time she wants Mexican food and who doesn't love that?

¾ cup cooked chicken (use rotisserie chicken or cook your own)
3 tablespoons of red enchilada sauce
¼ cup diced tomatoes and chilies (canned)
2 tablespoons water
2 (6-inch) flour tortillas cut into strips
½ cup shredded cheddar cheese
Guacamole (optional)

Heat skillet to 350°F. Add the chicken, enchilada sauce, tomatoes/green chilies and water to the skillet and heat for 2 minutes.

Add the tortilla strips and stir into the mixture. Turn off the heat and sprinkle with the cheese. Wait a minute before removing so cheese can melt. Top with guacamole.

West Virginia Chili Hot Dogs

If you haven't tasted chili on a hot dog you haven't lived (or at least you haven't lived in West Virginia.) Try this and you'll be a believer!

Beef wieners
½ cup water

Hot dog buns
Ketchup, mustard

Chili:
¼ pound ground beef
1   tablespoon chopped onion
½ teaspoon minced garlic
3   tablespoons ketchup
½ teaspoon cumin
½ teaspoon chili powder
½ teaspoon mustard

Heat skillet to 350°F and add ½ cup water. Put wiener in hot water and cook for 5 minutes, turning the wiener over a few times while cooking. Place wiener on plate and pour liquid out of skillet, if any is left. Cook ground beef and onion for 2 minutes stirring and flipping with the spatula to make sure it is cooked thoroughly. Add garlic, ketchup, cumin, chili powder and mustard and cook an additional minute.

Place wiener in the bun and put your ketchup and mustard, if desired, on the hot dog and add about 4 tablespoons of chili on top.

Sarah H. Long

Ramen Noodle Stir Fry

Every college student has to have ramen noodles in their room. They are so tasty and very inexpensive. This recipe uses the noodles and the flavor packet in a non-traditional way.

Package of ramen noodles (any flavor but the soy sauce flavor is extra good in this)
Package of frozen stir fry veggies (around 8 oz)
2 tablespoons canola or olive oil

Turn electric skillet to 400°F and heat 4 cups water to a boil with the lid covering the skillet (this takes about 3 to 4 minutes). Add the ramen, broken into a few pieces, and cook for about 2 ½ minutes (keep the flavor packet for later). Drain the water and put ramen noodles on a plate. Sprinkle ½ teaspoon of the flavor packet over the ramen and mix well. Heat 2 tablespoons of oil in the skillet. Add the frozen vegetables and another ½ teaspoon of the flavor packet over the veggies and cook 3-4 minutes. Pour cooked vegetables over the cooked ramen.

French Fries

Who doesn't love fresh hot french fries? This makes enough for 1 person so add more oil and 1 potato per person if you are feeding a crowd.

1 potato cut in slices
1 ½ cups canola oil
Ketchup, if desired
Salt

Put oil in skillet and heat to 350°F. After about 1 ½ minutes when oil is hot, add the potatoes. Cook for 5 minutes. Flip potatoes that may not be totally sub-merged in oil to make sure they are cooked evenly. Remove with a slotted spoon to drain the excess oil and place them on a few paper towels. Let drain and cool for a couple minutes then salt and enjoy dipped in ketchup.

Philly Cheese Steak

Cheese steaks are surprisingly easy to fix yourself. Much better than getting takeout and having a cold soggy sub in your room. Make your own and have it fresh and hot! Remember the butcher in the grocery store can cut meat thin for you and give you smaller pieces than what is out in the meat case. This makes enough for 2 subs.

1 teaspoon vegetable oil
¼ onion, sliced
1 green bell pepper, cut in strips
Sliced provolone or other cheese of your choice
2 sub rolls
½ pound of thinly sliced beefsteak (eye round or sirloin)
Dash of salt and pepper

Heat skillet to 350°F. Add oil and stir to coat bottom of skillet. Place meat in the skillet and season with a dash of salt and pepper. Cook each piece of meat 1 minute on each side. Add peppers and onions then cook about 1 minute more. Transfer meat and veggies to plate. Drain excess liquid and place sub rolls face down to toast quickly, about 30 seconds. Remove and immediately put cheese on sub rolls and add meat and veggies to further melt the cheese.

Margherita Pizza

My son loves Margherita pizza. He could live on these super simple pizza/quesadilla-like treats!

Tortillas

Can of Italian (basil, garlic, oregano) diced tomatoes
   (drained)
Shredded or sliced mozzarella cheese
Cooking spray

Heat electric skillet to 300°F. Spray bottom of pan
with cooking spray. Place tortilla in skillet and spoon
a few tablespoons of the canned tomatoes over the
tortilla. Top with a handful of mozzarella cheese and
top with another tortilla. Spray the tortilla with cooking oil spray. Cook for about 1 minute until cheese
melts. As it cooks, carefully flip the pizza over with
a spatula about every 20 seconds so one side does not
burn.

Grilled Chicken Caesar Salad

This is a one of my girl's favorites. She loves having this light but filling salad for lunch or dinner any day of the week.

½ cup raw chicken, cut into strips
½ cup Italian dressing
Olive oil
Romaine lettuce
Parmesan cheese–fresh is better but the dried kind is
  fine too
Italian or focaccia bread
Caesar dressing

Marinate the raw cut-up chicken in a bowl with ½ cup Italian dressing. Heat skillet to 300°F and add 1 tablespoon olive oil. Cut 2 slices of the Italian or focaccia bread and cook in olive oil for 30 seconds on each side. Remove from pan and cut into squares to make croutons.

Increase skillet temperature to 350°F and add another tablespoon of olive oil and cook the chicken for 5 minutes flipping the chicken a couple times to make sure both sides cook evenly. Wash and tear romaine lettuce on a plate. Add the croutons and chicken then sprinkle with parmesan cheese. Pour Caesar dressing on top.

Sarah H. Long

Chicken Alfredo Pasta

Sure, you can use jarred Alfredo sauce, but this is SO MUCH BETTER.

½ cup raw chicken, cut into pieces
Spaghetti noodles (when you hold them at one end it should be about the size of a nickel in diameter for each person)
3 tablespoons butter
1 + ½ teaspoons minced garlic
1 cup half and half or heavy whipping cream
⅓ cup a parmesan cheese

Turn skillet to 350°F and melt 1 tablespoon butter along with ½ teaspoon garlic. Add chicken and cook approximately 3 minutes until chicken is cooked through and no longer pink. Remove chicken from the skillet and set aside. Next cook the noodles by adding 2 ½ cups water to the skillet with the spaghetti (break noodles in half before adding to pan). Cover and simmer until pasta has softened, about 12 minutes. Add noodles to plate and empty any excess water from skillet.

Lower the skillet temperature to 250°F. Add 2 tablespoons of butter and 1 teaspoon of garlic to the pan. After butter has melted, add 1 cup half and half, ⅓ cup parmesan cheese and cook 2 more minutes. Add noodles and chicken back in pan and stir to coat. Salt and pepper to taste.

Spaghetti with Meatballs

To get one serving of spaghetti noodles, hold them together inside a clenched fist in your hand and one end should be about the diameter of a nickel.

1 serving of spaghetti noodles
Jar of spaghetti sauce

Meatball ingredients:
¼ pound ground round
½ tablespoon diced onion
½ tablespoon green pepper
1 slice of bread or toast, torn in small pieces OR 3 saltine crackers
1 tablespoon milk
1 teaspoon parmesan cheese
½ tablespoon ketchup
⅛ teaspoon salt
⅛ teaspoon pepper

Turn skillet to 350°F. Add 3 cups water, cover with lid and bring to a boil (about 3 minutes). Break spaghetti noodles in half before putting in the boiling water. Boil noodles with the lid closed about 8 minutes. When noodles are soft and fully cooked, drain the water and transfer noodles to a plate.

Combine all meatball ingredients into a bowl and form meatballs into about the size of golf balls. This makes about 7 or 8 meatballs.

In the empty skillet (still heated at 350°F) put the entire jar of spaghetti sauce and formed meatballs into skillet. Cook covered about 8-10 minutes. Meatballs should be cooked through (cut one in half to make sure they are done). Pour sauce and meatballs over noodles.

College Cooking 101: Fast Food Without a Kitchen

Shrimp & Sausage Veggie Stir Fry

I love a good stir fry. This one is heavy on protein to keep you energized for those late nights studying.

10 shrimp (or about ½ of a 12 oz bag) peeled
½ pound Polska Kielbasa or andouille sausage
1 medium zucchini, sliced
¼ cup sliced mushrooms
1 green or red bell pepper, chopped
3 tablespoons olive oil
1 tablespoon garlic and herb blend seasoning (found in spice section of store)

Heat skillet to 350°F. Pour olive oil and garlic and herb seasoning into the skillet and mix well. Add shrimp and sausage to pan and cook for 5 minutes, stirring and flipping with a spatula every minute or so to evenly cook. Add the vegetables and cook all together 6 minutes. Serve.

Easy Peasy Paella

I could totally be a vegetarian with more dishes like this. Yellow rice makes this dish super flavorful. Feel free to substitute/omit vegetables to your liking.

Package of yellow rice
¼ cup sliced mushrooms
1 sliced zucchini
1 sliced yellow squash
¼ cup frozen peas
½ small onion, chopped
2 tablespoons olive oil
Salt/pepper

Heat skillet to 350°F. Prepare yellow rice according to packet directions (adding water and cooking). Remove rice from skillet and place on plate. Add olive oil to skillet and cook the vegetables for 5 minutes. Sprinkle with a dash of salt and pepper as they cook. Mix rice in with the cooked vegetables and serve.

Shrimp and Broccoli Lo Mein

You can throw this meal together much faster than calling for takeout and waiting for delivery. Omit the shrimp for a vegetarian dish or substitute the shrimp for chicken or steak and make you own take out!

Lo mein or spaghetti noodles (I use spaghetti)

10 shrimp (or ½ of a 12 oz bag) peeled
2 tablespoons canola oil
1 cup of broccoli chopped
¼ cup chopped onion
1 teaspoon minced garlic

Mix together in bowl for sauce:
1 tablespoon dry sherry
3 tablespoons soy sauce
1 teaspoon light brown sugar
1 teaspoon sesame oil

Heat skillet to 350°F and boil water according to the noodle package directions. Cook noodles and drain the water. Place cooked noodles on a plate.

Heat 2 tablespoons of oil in skillet and cook shrimp for 2 minutes. Add broccoli, onion and garlic and cook 3 more minutes, stirring and flipping over to evenly cook. Stir in sauce and noodles and heat through about 1 minute before serving.

Pad Thai

I've never met a college student who didn't like Thai food...

4 ounces dried, flat rice noodles
2 teaspoon vegetable oil
1 tablespoon brown sugar
1 tablespoon lime juice
1 ½ tablespoons soy sauce
Dash of Sriracha, optional
1 green onion, sliced
1 teaspoon minced garlic
¼ cup fresh cilantro
1 tablespoon chopped peanuts

Soak noodles in water according to package directions, typically around 15 minutes, then drain. In a separate bowl, mix together brown sugar, lime juice, soy sauce, and Sriracha, if using.

Heat 1 teaspoon oil in skillet to 350°F and cook green onion and garlic 1 minute. Add noodles and cook, tossing with a spatula until noodles are soft, about 1 minute. If noodles are not soft, like cooked spaghetti, you may need to add a couple of tablespoons of water and cook a minute more until they are soft. Add sauce and cook additional minute. Top with cilantro and peanuts.

Sarah H. Long

Slow Cooker

A mini slow cooker can be a life saver. There is nothing like coming home to a warm dinner after a long afternoon of lectures or band practice. As the appliance name implies, food is cooked low and slow. This type of cooking takes a few minutes of preparation several hours prior to the meal (think planning for dinner after lunch). The preparation pays off in having a dinner ready to eat right out of the slow cooker when you get home.

Contrary to popular thinking, slow cooker meals cannot be cooked all day long or the food will be transformed into a leather-like texture. A few hours is generally the perfect cook time for perfect results. Pay attention to the cooking times so you can have juicy, fall-off-the-bone meat that will be some of the best you have ever tasted! Putting frozen meat in can give you an extra hour of cooking time.

Several of the smaller slow cookers are warmers that heat lunches up but do not actually cook food. Make sure you purchase one that has a warm, low and high setting. Please note that all these recipes are for the small slow cookers (1.5 to 2 quart size), not the regular family size, and the ingredients have been adjusted accordingly.

Sarah H. Long

Slow Cooker Lasagna

The ultimate comfort food. If you've had a bad day or just need the warmth of a good meal this one always lifts your spirits. Great with a couple slices of crusty bread.

The trick to this recipe is that the lasagna noodles are cooked by layering sauce and cheese around them (not boiling in water as their package says) -so make sure there is plenty of sauce to surround the noodles.

Lasagna noodles, uncooked
1 jar of spaghetti sauce
15 or 16 oz. ricotta cheese
1 egg
1 teaspoon Italian seasoning
Small bag of shredded mozzarella cheese
Shredded parmesan cheese

Spoon about ½ cup sauce onto the bottom of the slow cooker. Break one lasagna noodle into 3 pieces to fit the bottom layer of the slow cooker. In a separate bowl mix the container of ricotta with the egg and 1 teaspoon Italian seasoning. Layer ½ cup of the ricotta mixture over the noodles. Place the next layers as follows:

¼ cup mozzarella cheese
2 tablespoons parmesan cheese

1 lasagna shell broken into pieces
¾ cup sauce
½ cup ricotta mixture
¼ cup mozzarella cheese
2 tablespoons parmesan cheese

Cook on low for 3 hours. Do not overcook or cook on high.

Sarah H. Long

Slow Cooker "Grilled" Chicken

This tastes like the grilled chicken at fast food restaurants.

¼ cup Italian dressing
Uncooked chicken breast
Bun, tortilla or wrap of your choice
Mayonnaise and lettuce if you like

Put uncooked chicken breast in slow cooker and pour ¼ cup Italian dressing over it and cover with lid. Cook on low for 3 hours (preferred method for extra juiciness) or on high for 1½ hours. Put chicken on bread of your choice with mayonnaise and lettuce if desired.

Potato Soup

I can't think of anything better to come home to on a rainy or snowy day (or any day actually) than potato soup. Makes about 2-3 servings.

1 large potato, diced
2 tablespoons of diced onion
1 ⅓ cups chicken broth
1 garlic cloves minced
1 ½ tablespoons butter
⅓ cup half and half
⅓ cup cheddar cheese
Dash of salt and pepper

Mix first five ingredients in slow cooker. Cook on low 4 ½-5 hours or high 3 hours. Stir in half and half and cheese then serve in mugs or bowls.

Hawaiian Chicken

Yes pineapple juice is good for more than just making piña coladas (lol). It is my go-to marinade. I buy a small pack of the cans of pineapple juice as opposed to a large jar because you can keep the unopened ones without refrigeration to save for later use.

6 oz. pineapple juice (1 small can) (almost 1 cup)
2 tablespoons soy sauce

Place a chicken breast or two in the slow cooker. Mix pineapple juice and soy sauce together in a bowl and add on top of chicken. Cook on low 3 hours (my preference) or high 1 ½ hours. Great alone, on a bed of salad greens, or served on a bun with a slice of pineapple.

Chocolate Molten Lava Fudge Cake

*This cake will knock your socks off – it's that good!
Serve this to your roommate after a bad breakup or
make it for yourself because you deserve it!
This serves about 4 people. It pairs perfectly with a
scoop of vanilla ice cream.*

1 cup from a box of chocolate cake mix
1 tablespoon + 1 ¼ teaspoons vegetable oil
1/3 cup water
1 egg
3 tablespoons + 1 ½ teaspoons from a package of chocolate instant pudding
2/3 cup milk
1/3 cup of semi-sweet chocolate chips

Mix cake mix with the oil, water and egg together in the bottom of the slow cooker. In a separate bowl combine pudding with milk then pour over cake mix. Sprinkle the top with chocolate chips. Cook on high for 2 ½ hours. Cake will have some liquid on top which makes it like hot fudge over the cake.

Buffalo Chicken Dip

Bring this to a tailgate or invite your suite-mates to share this for a study break.

2 cans (12.5 oz) white chunk chicken
8 oz cream cheese (cut this up to melt faster)
½ cup buffalo hot sauce (Frank's Red Hot or store brand is fine)
¾ cup shredded cheddar cheese
½ cup ranch or blue cheese dressing
Tortilla chips

Combine first five ingredients and stir. Cook on low for 1 hour and 15 minutes. Use tortilla chips for dipping.

Street Tacos

These are super popular at restaurants and are sold in food trucks and carts in bigger cities. Make your own at home with a few simple ingredients.

1 lb. steak cut in strips (flank steak works well)
½ of an onion, cut in strips
1 green pepper, cut in strips
2 tablespoons orange juice
2 tablespoons lime juice
3 tablespoons soy sauce
1 tablespoon olive oil
½ teaspoon sugar
2 ½ tablespoons chopped garlic
½ tablespoon cumin
½ tablespoon chili powder
Flour tortillas
Toppings of your choice: guacamole, sour cream, cilantro

Put steak, onion and green pepper in the slow cooker. Mix together in a separate bowl the orange juice, lime juice, soy sauce, olive oil, sugar, garlic, cumin and chili powder. Pour over steak. Cook on low 3 hours or high for 2 hours. Serve in tortillas with your choice of toppings.

Pumpkin Spice Latte

Your mom called and said your credit card bill was too high because you were buying too many lattes at the campus coffee shop. Make your own lattes and invite a couple friends over or use this to keep you fueled for a long night of studying. This recipe makes about 3 servings. You can refrigerate and reheat in the microwave the next day.

2 cups strong brewed coffee
2 cups milk
¼ cup sugar
¼ teaspoon pumpkin spice seasoning
½ cup canned pumpkin
½ tablespoon vanilla
Can of whipped cream for top (if desired)

Combine all ingredients in slow cooker (except whipped cream). Cook on high until hot about 1 hour. Serve with whipped cream on top if desired.

Sarah H. Long

Paradise Caribbean Jerk Chicken

Imagine you are in a tropical paradise instead of studying in your room. Maybe this recipe will help put you in that frame of mind...

1 chicken breast
¾ cup water
½ bottle of Caribbean jerk marinade
1 green bell pepper, cut in strips
½ small sweet onion, sliced into strips
Flour tortillas
Shredded cheddar cheese
Salsa (the fresher kind in the deli section of the grocery store is best!)

Place chicken, water, marinade, onion and peppers in the slow cooker. Cook on low 3 hours or high 1½ hours. Spoon onto flour tortillas and top with grated cheese and salsa.

Barbecue Chicken Sliders

It doesn't get any easier than this recipe and it is so good.

1 chicken breast
Dash of salt and pepper

¼ cup barbecue sauce
2 tablespoons water
Slider buns

Put chicken breast in slow cooker and salt and pepper to season. Put ¼ cup barbecue sauce on top of chicken along with 2 tablespoons water. Cook on low for 3 hours or high for 1½ hours. Put on slider buns and enjoy!

Party Lil' Smokies

These would be perfect for a study group party.

1 package cocktail sausages (around 14 oz)
½ cup barbecue sauce
¼ cup plus 2 tablespoons grape jelly

Dump all ingredients in slow cooker and cook on low for 2 hours. Serve with sweet Hawaiian rolls or they are great on their own!

Pizza Dip

Sometimes you need a snack that will fill you up and can serve as a meal as well.

Cooking spray
4 oz cream cheese
½ jar pizza sauce
½ package shredded mozzarella or pizza blend cheese
¼ cup shredded parmesan
1 tablespoon Italian seasoning
Toast, crackers or tortilla chips for dipping

Spray slow cooker with cooking spray. Combine cream cheese, pizza sauce and mozzarella. Sprinkle parmesan on top. Cook on low 3 hours or on high 1 hour and 15 minutes. Serve with toast, crackers or tortilla chips for dipping.

Steel Cut Strawberry Oatmeal

Instant oatmeal is good too but nothing beats steel cut oats for flavor, nutrition and taste.

Cooking spray
1 cup water
½ cup sliced strawberries
6 tablespoons steel cut oats
1 teaspoon vanilla extract
1 tablespoon sugar

Spray slow cooker then add remaining ingredients and stir to combine. Cook on low for about 4 hours.

Chicken and Dumplings

This is comfort food at its finest. Put this on after lunch to have for dinner.

2 uncooked chicken tenderloins or 1 chicken breast
½ can of cream of chicken soup
¾ cup of chicken broth
¾ cup frozen peas and carrots
1 small can of biscuits (6 oz)

Put the first four ingredients in the slow cooker and mix. Cook on high for 2 hours then add the biscuits (each one torn in half) on top of the mixture pushing each dough ball down so the liquid is slightly covering. Cook on high an additional 1 hour.

Cinnamon Roll Breakfast Bake

I have never met a cinnamon roll I didn't like. This is one of my favorites.

Cooking spray
1 12 oz can refrigerated cinnamon rolls
1 egg
¼ cup whipping cream
1 tablespoon maple syrup
¼ teaspoon vanilla
½ teaspoon cinnamon
Frosting from the cinnamon roll package

Spray slow cooker with cooking spray. Layer cinnamon rolls in bottom of slow cooker. Stack some of top of another. In a bowl mix together the egg, whipping cream, maple syrup, vanilla and cinnamon. Pour this mixture over the cinnamon rolls. Cover and cook on high 2 hours. To serve, scoop the cinnamon rolls out onto a plate and then drizzle some of the frosting over each piece.

Toaster Oven

This is for much more than just making toast! Think mini-oven!

Copy Cat Chick-Fil-A Sandwich

This is my family's favorite meal–hands down. It is close enough to the original to satisfy our craving.

1 small chicken breast
3 tablespoons dill pickle juice (buy a small jar of cheap dill slices and pour some out)
¼ cup milk
1 egg
6 tablespoons flour
¼ cup breadcrumbs
½ tablespoon season salt, such as Lawry's
¼ teaspoon black pepper
Cooking oil spray

Put raw chicken in a zipper seal bag with pickle juice for about an hour. In a small mixing bowl, whisk together milk and egg. In another bowl add flour and roll chicken in the flour to cover generously on all sides. Next dip the chicken in the egg/milk mixture. Then roll it in a mixture of breadcrumbs and season with salt and pepper. Spray with cooking spray and bake in a preheated oven at 425°F for 20 minutes. Serve on top of a toasted round bun and add pickle slices.

Portobello Pesto Burgers

Portobello mushrooms are vegetables that taste almost like meat. It's something different instead of the same old hamburger. This recipe makes 2 burgers.

1 tablespoon olive oil
½ tablespoon balsamic vinegar
Dash of salt
Dash of pepper
2 large portobello mushrooms, stems removed
2 slices mozzarella cheese
2 round sandwich rolls (Italian or Kaiser)
1 tablespoon purchased pesto
¼ cup mayonnaise

In a bowl combine olive oil, vinegar, salt and pepper. Using a utensil remove the gills and stems from the underside of the mushroom. Preheat toaster to 400°F. Rub the olive oil mixture on one side of the mushrooms and cook 4 minutes. Turn the mushrooms over, spread more mixture and cook 4 more minutes. Remove mushrooms onto a plate. Toast bun face side up and melt cheese on one side. Mix pesto and mayonnaise together then spread on side without cheese. Assemble sandwich by putting a mushroom in the middle of the two bun slices.

Sarah H. Long

Pepperoni Rolls

A West Virginia classic, these are a perfect tailgating snack before the game! Your friends will make sure you get an invite every time if you promise to bring these!

Bag of frozen bread dough rolls (such as Rhodes brand)
Stick pepperoni

Let 8 frozen dough balls thaw on the toaster oven tray until double (about 4 hours). Cut pepperoni into two inch sticks. Wrap pepperoni inside rolls so there is no pepperoni showing and let rise another hour. Bake at 400°F for 15 minutes. Let cool before serving and store at room temperature.

Naan Pizza

These were my brother's favorite growing up. He used to eat them for breakfast but I think they make a great quick lunch or dinner.

1 slice of naan bread
3 tablespoons pizza sauce (spaghetti sauce works well too)
½ cup shredded mozzarella cheese
Pepperoni and other pizza toppings of your choice

Preheat oven to 400°F. Spread pizza sauce on top of naan. Top with mozzarella cheese and any other toppings of your choice. Bake at 400°F for about 8 minutes.

Grilled Cheese (just like mom used to make)

My grandmother use to make these for me when I came over to visit. Comfort food at its finest!

2 slices of bread of your choice (I love Pepperidge Farm white thins for this)
2 slices of Colby, cheddar or American cheese

1 teaspoon butter

Adjust rack to bottom position. Preheat the oven to 400°F. Butter one side of each piece of bread and place face down onto the baking sheet. Put cheese on each slice. Bake at 400°F for 6 minutes and put the slices cheese-side together to form the sandwich.

Toaster Salmon

When my husband and I first got married we made this in the toaster all the time. Very simple and very tasty.

2 pieces of salmon
½ tablespoon soy sauce
½ tablespoon ginger
½ tablespoon cooking sherry (find this in stores near vinegars)
2 tablespoons butter, melted

Mix soy sauce, ginger, cooking sherry and butter together in a bowl. Spoon mixture over salmon steaks and heat on broil about 15 minutes. Make sure the salmon is 3 to 4 inches away from the top heating element.

Open Face Tuna Melts

This classic sandwich is always a hit for lunch, dinner or a study break.

Can of tuna, drained of liquid
½ teaspoon lemon juice
2 tablespoons chopped celery
2 tablespoons of mayonnaise
English muffins or bread of your choice
Swiss cheese

Mix together in a bowl tuna, lemon juice, celery and mayonnaise. Split and toast English muffins lightly and remove from toaster. Place two tablespoons of tuna mixture on each muffin. Place a slice of Swiss on each and broil for 3-4 minutes until cheese is bubbly.

Indoor S'mores

Invite a few friends to join you for indoor s'mores tonight! For a new twist, add fresh sliced strawberries in between the chocolate and marshmallow layer.

Graham crackers

Bag of jumbo marshmallows
Hershey chocolate bars

Make sure you adjust the rack and tray to the lowest setting possible. There needs to be plenty of space between the heating element and the top of the marshmallows.

Turn the toaster on broil. Line the tray/baking sheet with foil. Break graham crackers apart into large squares and place them onto the baking sheet. I fit 6 graham crackers on my toaster tray. Put a square of chocolate on the graham cracker and a marshmallow on top. Broil 2 to 3 minutes watching carefully the entire cooking time. Remove the s'more from the oven and add the top layer of graham cracker.

Bean Burritos

What college student passes up a burrito? Make this in your room quicker than you can go out and get one at a drive-thru.

Cooking oil spray
Flour tortillas
1 can of black beans, rinsed and drained (or refried beans work too with no rinsing/draining)
1 can of corn, drained
⅓ cup cheddar or Mexican blend cheese
Toppings such as guacamole, salsa

Preheat oven to 400°F. Spray baking sheet with cooking oil spray. Place tortilla on a plate and put about ¼ cup drained black beans and a spoonful of corn onto the tortilla. Top with cheese and roll into a burrito. Spray the top of the burrito with cooking oil spray. Bake at 400°F for about 10 minutes. It is done when the tortilla is slightly browning on top and the cheese is melted inside.

Cinnamon Toast

This recipe reminds me of what my mom would fix me when we ran out of Pop-Tarts at home when I was a kid. It beats those any day.

2 slices of your favorite bread
1 tablespoon of sugar
¼ teaspoon cinnamon
Butter

Butter your favorite bread. In a separate bowl mix the sugar and cinnamon together. Spread on top of buttered bread. Toast and enjoy!

Hot Italian Sub

No need to go to the sub shop today. Make these yourself!

Sub rolls
2 slices of salami
Few slices pepperoni
1 slice ham
¼ cup mozzarella cheese
About 8 banana pepper rings

Place sub rolls flat side up in toaster. Put meat slices and pepper rings on one half and put cheese on the other half. Toast and serve.

Ham, Brie & Apple Sandwich

This sandwich brings a few unexpected ingredients together to form the perfect match!

Bread of your choice – artisan bread works well
2 slices deli ham
2 slices of brie (or any other cheese you like)
4 very thin green apple slices

Place bread with flat side up in toaster. On one side put ham and on the other put apple slices with sliced brie on top. Toast until cheese has melted. Put both halves together and serve.

Buffalo Party Wings

My son could eat wings for any meal. These are quick and easy and would be great when you invite your friends over to watch the game. These are very inexpensive which makes them a college student's dream food.

Wing drumettes (fresh or thawed if frozen)
Dash of salt
Dash of pepper
Dash of garlic powder
1 tablespoon parmesan cheese
3 tablespoons of red hot sauce (such as Frank's)
1 tablespoon butter for each wing

Line the toaster tray with aluminum foil. Place as many chicken drumettes as you can on the tray without overlapping. Sprinkle a dash of salt, pepper and garlic powder on each wing. Sprinkle parmesan cheese on each one as well. Pour about ½ tablespoon of hot sauce over each piece. Top each drumette with 1 tablespoon of butter. Bake at 425°F for 25 minutes.

Bruschetta

This recipe takes a few simple ingredients and makes a wonderful meal!

1 large tomato, chopped
2 tablespoons chopped sweet onion
1 tablespoons olive oil
½ teaspoon dried oregano
½ teaspoon fresh basil (not dried – this is important!)
Grated fresh parmesan cheese (buy in a bag with shredded cheeses or in deli section – this is not the dried kind you put on spaghetti)
Loaf of Italian bread cut into 1 inch slices

Put the slices of bread in the toaster and lightly toast. Remove and preheat toaster oven to 400°F. Mix in a bowl the tomatoes, onion, olive oil, oregano and basil. Top the bread with this mixture and sprinkle parmesan cheese on top. Cook for 7 minutes.

Sarah H. Long

Sausage and Peppers

Yes, you can make a great meal like this in your toaster oven.

2 brats or sausage of your choice
½ sweet onion, sliced
1 bell pepper
Salt and pepper
¼ teaspoon dried basil
2 tablespoon butter

Preheat toaster oven to 400°F. Line the tray with aluminum foil. Place brats, onions and peppers on tray and sprinkle basil, salt and pepper over them. Cut up butter and scatter on top. Cook for 15 minutes.

Sarah H. Long

Blender

If you enjoy smoothies or protein drinks at home this is a must have! Get creative with blending a meal to drink on your way to class.

Strawberry Smoothie

This reminds me of the famous strawberry drinks served at a national coffee chain. But unlike those, these are good for you!!!

1 ¼ cup frozen strawberries
3 tablespoons plain Greek yogurt
1 tablespoon peanut butter or almond butter
2 teaspoons honey or agave
1 ½ teaspoon vanilla extract
1 cup regular or almond milk

Blend all ingredients together. You can refrigerate this up to 24 hours.

Banana Protein Drink

Great for mornings on the go or after a workout.

1 cup milk (regular or almond)
½ cup Greek yogurt (plain or vanilla)
1 scoop vanilla protein powder (you can omit if it's
    not your thing)
1 frozen banana

Blend all ingredients together.

Healthy Peanut Butter Banana Ice Cream

This is actually not ice cream but tastes like it. The trick is the frozen banana that simulates the texture of ice cream to perfection.

3 bananas
2 tablespoons peanut butter
¼ teaspoon vanilla extract
Dash of cinnamon

Cut bananas into small chunks and freeze until solid, at least 1-2 hours. Add bananas to blender with peanut butter, vanilla and cinnamon. These will be like ice cubes and you may have to stir a few times, but the result is a creamy ice cream texture.

Healthy Shamrock Shake

Every year in March my kids and I rush to our near-est fast food restaurant to get a Shamrock Shake. Here is a much healthier version that tastes great!

½ cup fat free, 1% or almond milk
3 peeled bananas, frozen

5-7 baby spinach leaves
½ teaspoon peppermint extract
1 tablespoon mini chocolate chips

Blend until smooth.

Kale Apple Smoothie

This recipe is super yummy and unlike many smoothies does not contain a banana.

1 cup baby kale
1 large apple (peeled and cut in pieces)
2 tablespoons maple syrup
Juice of ½ of a lemon
¾ cup almond milk (or other milk)
2 teaspoons flax seed
5 ice cubes

Blend all ingredients together.

Vanilla Chai Smoothie

Chai drinks are very popular at coffee restaurants. Try this one in your own room.

½ cup vanilla almond milk
½ cup cold black tea
1 ½ banana
1 tablespoon vanilla protein powder (or vanilla extract)
¼ teaspoon ground cinnamon
⅛ teaspoon ground cardamom

Blend all ingredients together.

Blueberry Green Tea Smoothie

Green tea revs up your metabolism and gives you lots of energy. What college student doesn't need that?

1 cup of green tea (brewed and sweetened to your liking), room temperature or chilled

1 ½ cup frozen blueberries
½ banana
¾ cup vanilla soy or almond milk

Blend all ingredients together.

Peanut Butter and Jelly Smoothie

This is sooooo good and much easier to take to class than the sandwich.

1 cup almond milk
2 ½ tablespoons peanut butter
1 frozen banana
1 ½ cups frozen strawberries

Blend all ingredients together.

Skinny Frosty

My kids and I love a Wendy's chocolate Frosty. This is a much healthier version.

¾ cup almond milk
15 ice cubes
½ teaspoon vanilla extract
2 tablespoons cocoa powder
⅓ banana
1 tablespoon honey or sugar (can be omitted if limiting sugar)

Blend all ingredients together.

Cold Prevention Smoothie

One of the worst things you will experience your freshman year is that first cold without your mom to care for you. Make this to ward off the evil cold viruses lurking around.

1 banana, frozen
1 cup frozen peaches
½ cup yogurt, Greek or almond is yummy
½ teaspoon ground ginger
¼ teaspoon ground turmeric
1 cup orange juice

Blend all ingredients together.

Keurig Recipes

Every college student needs a Keurig machine or other "pod" style coffee maker. They brew great cups of coffee and hot tea with purchased pods. But have you considered what you can make from just the hot water it generates? Before trying these recipes, run a test mug of water through the machine to clear away any spare coffee grounds.

Sarah H. Long

Hot Chocolate (with ideas on how to spice it up!)

A warm mug of hot chocolate is almost as good as a hug from home. Enjoy a cup today in your room.

Envelope of hot chocolate (like Swiss Miss)
Cup of hot water from the Keurig
Marshmallows or marshmallow cream

Mix the first two ingredients and stir well. Add marshmallows or marshmallow cream on top.

Other ideas for mix-ins:
   *Peanut butter for added flavor and protein
   *A sprinkle of cinnamon on top
   *Nutella
   *An Oreo or two
   *Round peppermint candy or candy cane
   *Maple syrup with nutmeg sprinkled on top
   *Raspberry syrup and white chocolate chips
   *Caramel syrup

Southern Style Sweet Tea

My college-aged daughter loves sweet tea. Any tea lover will tell you sweet tea must be fresh-brewed and that the sugar must be dissolved in it while the brew is hot, not added afterwards to unsweetened tea that is cold...

1 Keurig K-Cup of any black tea
1 ¾ tablespoons sugar
Ice

Put the sugar in a mug, brew the hot tea and pour it directly over the sugar. Stir until the sugar is dissolved. Let sit until it is room temperature (or cover and refrigerate). Fill a glass with ice and pour the tea into the glass.

Sarah H. Long

Oatmeal

There is nothing like a bowl of oatmeal to warm you up and start your day off right. It's not just for breakfast anymore – makes a great lunch or dinner too!

½ cup quick 1 minute oats
1 cup of hot water from Keurig

Combine both ingredients in a bowl and mix well. For toppings I suggest cinnamon sugar blend (found in the spice section), agave or maple syrup, and fresh fruit such as strawberries or blueberries.

Mashed Potatoes

Adding bacon, chives or sour cream to these potatoes really makes them a meal.

1 cup of instant potato flakes
1 cup of hot water from the Keurig
¼ teaspoon salt
1 ½ tablespoons butter
½ cup milk

Run a cup of water from the Keurig and place in a bowl. Add the salt and butter; stir until melted. Add cold milk and the potato flakes. Stir so they absorb the liquid. Let sit for a few seconds then stir again to make extra fluffy.

Just Add Water Soup

It does not get any easier than this. Hope this helps you on a day where you are short on time but need a good hot meal.

1 "cup of soup" package or Ramen bowl of soup
1 cup of hot water from the Keurig

Stir well to combine.

Mocha Overnight Oats

This is coffee and breakfast in one! Eat on your way to class.

½ cup old fashioned oats
1 ½ teaspoons chia seeds
½ cup Greek yogurt
¼ cup chocolate milk
¼ cup brewed coffee, cooled to room temperature

Combine all of the above in a bowl and mix well. Place in the refrigerator overnight (or at least 6 hours).

Jello with Fruit

My kids have always loved Jello. Mix this up with different flavors of gelatin and stir in some fruit.

Box of gelatin (Jello) any flavor (my favorite is cherry)
1 cup hot water from Keurig
1 cup cold water
½ cup of fruit of your choice (bananas, berries, etc.)
Whipped cream (if desired)

In a bowl combine the powered gelatin package with the cup of hot water from the Keurig. Stir 2 minutes or until the powder is completely dissolved. Stir in the cold water. Place in individual cups or a baking dish and mix in fruit of your choice. Refrigerate until firm (about 4 hours). It is great served with whipped cream on top!

Stuffing

My favorite part of Thanksgiving is the stuffing. But it doesn't have to be a holiday to enjoy this tasty dish. It makes a great side dish or lunch!

¼ cup water
½ tablespoon margarine or butter
½ cup stuffing mix (such as Stove Top brand)

Brew a mug of hot water in the Keurig. Measure out ¼ cup of the hot water in a bowl and add the butter, stirring to dissolve. Add the stuffing mix and stir to combine.

Caramel Brulee Latte

Coffee is a necessity for many college students. Pass up the pricey coffee shop on campus and make this yourself to save lots of money!

1 brewed cup of strong black coffee
2 tablespoons caramel syrup
2 tablespoons of whipped cream

Brew your cup of strong coffee in the Keurig. Mix in 2 tablespoons of caramel drink syrup. Add whipped cream and stir. Top with more whipped cream and drizzle with caramel sauce.

Appendix

Ideas for Snacks to Have on Hand

Fruit – strawberries, apples, oranges, grapes (can be
    frozen)
Prepared salads
Peanut butter with bread, crackers, pretzels, celery
Hazelnut spread with bread or pretzels
Hummus with pretzels
Breakfast/cereal bars
Cereal
Instant oatmeal
Cans of soup
Ramen noodles
Hot chocolate packets (just add water!)
Microwave popcorn
Crackers
Potato chips (individual snack bags are nice as they
    stay fresh)
Yogurt
Raisins and nuts
Cheese sticks
Chips and salsa
Tuna

College Packing List

Bedroom:
- Sheets, bedspread/comforter, blankets
- Pillows –at least 2 for sleeping/studying, you may want throw pillows as well
- Lamp –one for the desk area and maybe another if overhead lighting is poor
- Hangers*
- Laundry basket –a tall one on wheels is helpful
- Clothes –shorts, shirts, pants/jeans, dresses, underwear, bras, sweaters, socks, shoes
- Small stick vacuum –typically around $20
- Small plastic dresser drawers on wheels –consider having this for school supplies and extra drawer space.
- Organizing boxes/containers –great for socks and other smaller items *
- Trash can – consider buying 2 (one for the bedroom and one for bathroom)*
- Tissues*
- Computer
- Power strip
- TV
- Coaxial cable to connect your TV – you might need a really long one depending on where you want the TV and where the cable wall plug is.
- Printer – optional as there may be one in the lobby of your dorm or library but some people prefer the convenience in their room

Bathroom:
- Shower products –shampoo, conditioner, soaps, etc.
- Shower curtain and liner
- Hairbrush, comb, curling iron, etc.
- Shaving supplies
- Trash can*
- Toilet paper
- Toilet brush
- Plunger*
- Cleaners –antibacterial wipes, toilet cleaner, shower cleaner*
- Air freshener*
- First aid kit – Band-Aids, cold medicine, ibuprofen, allergy medicine
- Laundry soap (pods or liquid), dryer sheets, stain remover spray
- Towels – 2 bath, 2 hand, and 2 washcloths
- Hand soap*
- Sunscreen
- Cosmetics

Kitchen:
- Silverware – plastic and metal
- Plates – paper and/or plastic*
- Plastic cups*
- Napkins*
- Zip seal bags to keep food fresh and use in fridge*
- Drinks-bottled water, soda, coffee
- Dishrags/dishtowels*
- Dishwashing liquid*

- Sponges*
- Clips for chips*
- Coffee maker
- Set of measuring cups, spoons*
- Spatula and slotted spoon*
- This book!

School supplies:
- Scientific calculator
- Scissors*
- Stapler (mini stapler is ideal!)*
- Tape*
- Pens, pencils, and highlighters*
- Planner/agenda -yes you need one! You have to stay organized and you don't have anyone else that will remind you when things are due or happening.
- Notebooks – loose leaf or spiral binders.
- Loose-leaf notebook paper
- Printer paper – You can usually print a lot of places on campus, but you have to provide your own paper.

Miscellaneous:
- Rain items (coat, umbrella, boots)
- Winter items (coat, gloves, hat, boots)
- Bathing suit
- Wall decorations
- Folding chair (soccer chair in a bag or softer plush one so friends won't have to sit on your bed)
- Command strips and hooks

- Sunglasses
- Hats
- Phone and laptop chargers
- Earphones*
- Cash
- Medical/Insurance Card
- Prescriptions
- Water bottle
- Coffee mug*
- Travel mug-to take hot drinks to class

*Can be purchased at your nearest dollar store

Note: The best advice for what to move all these items in are the large blue zippered bags from IKEA. Many people use the large hard plastic tubs with lids and they don't pack well in the car and are cumbersome to carry. The blue IKEA bags can be stacked on top of one another and can be carried in on your back with the straps. Store them under your bed for easy move out.

About the Author

Sarah H. Long is a mother of three, including one current and another soon-to-be college student. She graduated Phi Beta Kappa from Marietta College. A licensed CPA, she is the Chief Financial Officer and Assistant Cabinet Secretary of Administration for the State of West Virginia. Sarah lives with her husband Jimmy less than a mile from where she grew up in Charleston, West Virginia.

CPSIA information can be obtained
at www.ICGtesting.com
Printed in the USA
BVHW021837070521
606800BV00008B/23/J